Grandmother's memory book

This book was written by:

Grandma, tell me your story!

Memories and keepsakes for grandchild

© Copyrights 2021 - All rights reserved

You may not reproduce, duplicate or send the contents of this book without direct written permission from the author. You cannot hereby despite any circumstance blame the publisher or hold him or her te legal responsibility for any reparation, compensation or monetary forfeiture owing to the information included herein, either in a direct or indirect way.

Legal Notice: This book has copyright protection. You can use the book for personal purpose. You should not sell, use, alter, distribute, quote, take excerpts or paraphrase in part of whole the material contained in this book without obtaining the permission of the author first.

Disclaimer Notice: You must take note that the information in this document is for casual reading and entertainment purpose only. We have made every attempt to provide accurate, up to date and reliable information. We do not express or imply guarantees of any kind. The person who read admit that the writer is not occupied in giving legal, financial, medical or other advice. We put this book content by sourcing various places.

Please consult a licensed professional before you try any techniques shown in this book. By going through this document, the book lover comes to an agreement that under no situation is the author accountable for any forfeiture, direct or indirect, which they may incur because of the use of material contained in this document, including, but not limited to, - errors, omissions, or inaccuracies.

Contents:

Introduction – A note from the Author

Chapter 1 – My grandmother and her family

Chapter 2 – My grandmother growing up

Chapter 3 – Grandma becoming an adult

Chapter 4 – About Grandma's kids

Chapter 5 – Family traditions

Chapter 6 – About life and leaving

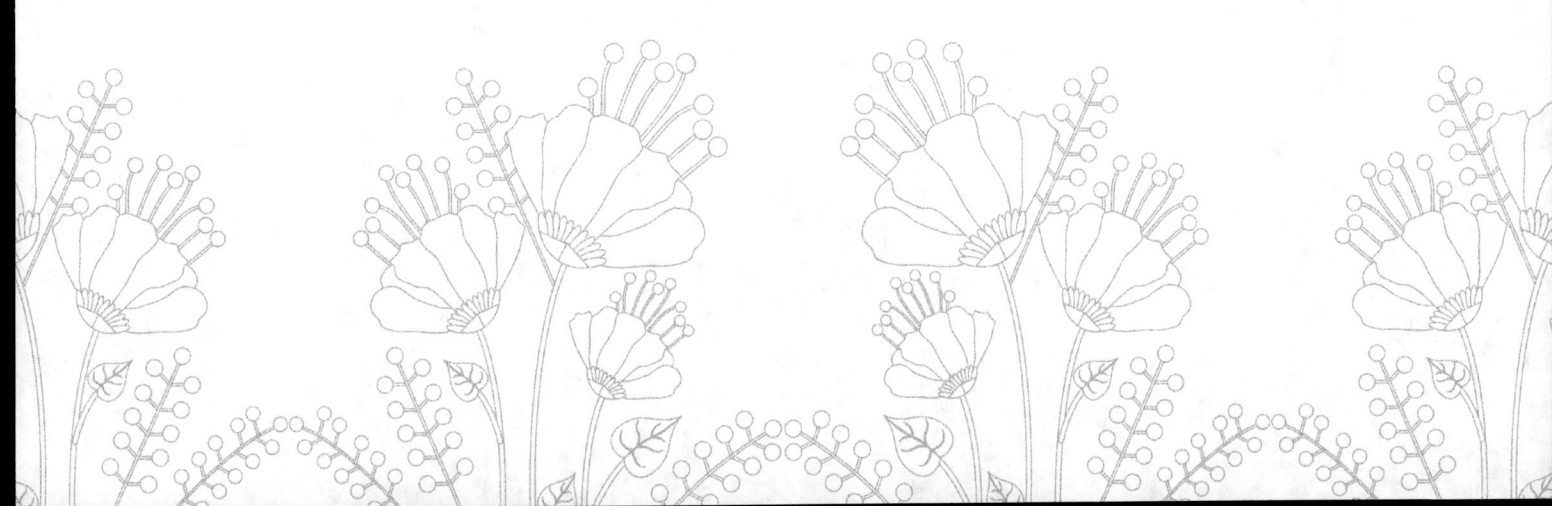

Introduction
A note to Grandmother from the Author

There is nobody quite like grandparents! Grandparents are a wonderful woman and man who slipped us sweets and let us get away with things our parents never would have agreed to. Beyond the extra treats and birthday gifts, grandparents offer younger generations a wealth of intriguing insights, gleaned from decades of real-life experience.

I lost my grandparents when I was a kid and I realize now, when I'm a parent myself, that there is so much I would like to know about my family. As I have kids myself and my parents are now grandparents, I realized that this is the perfect moment to record the memories of my parents for their grandchildren.

This journal was created for all and each of you grandmothers - both biological and non-biological - to capture and share the moments that have shaped your life. The journal includes engaging questions from a curious grandkid mind, which are meant to guide you on your road to writing your life story.

Once completed, this book will be a special keepsake of memories; it will be what your family learn about you when your journey ends. It's your chance to inspire the next generation and the generations to come with your experiences, accomplishments, and life lessons.

Even if you don't realize it yet, this journal is your family history. It's the story that you would like your loved ones to have and read one day. And on that day, we all realize that the ones we love never go away, they walk beside us ... unseen, unheard, yet always near, still loved, still missed and very dear.

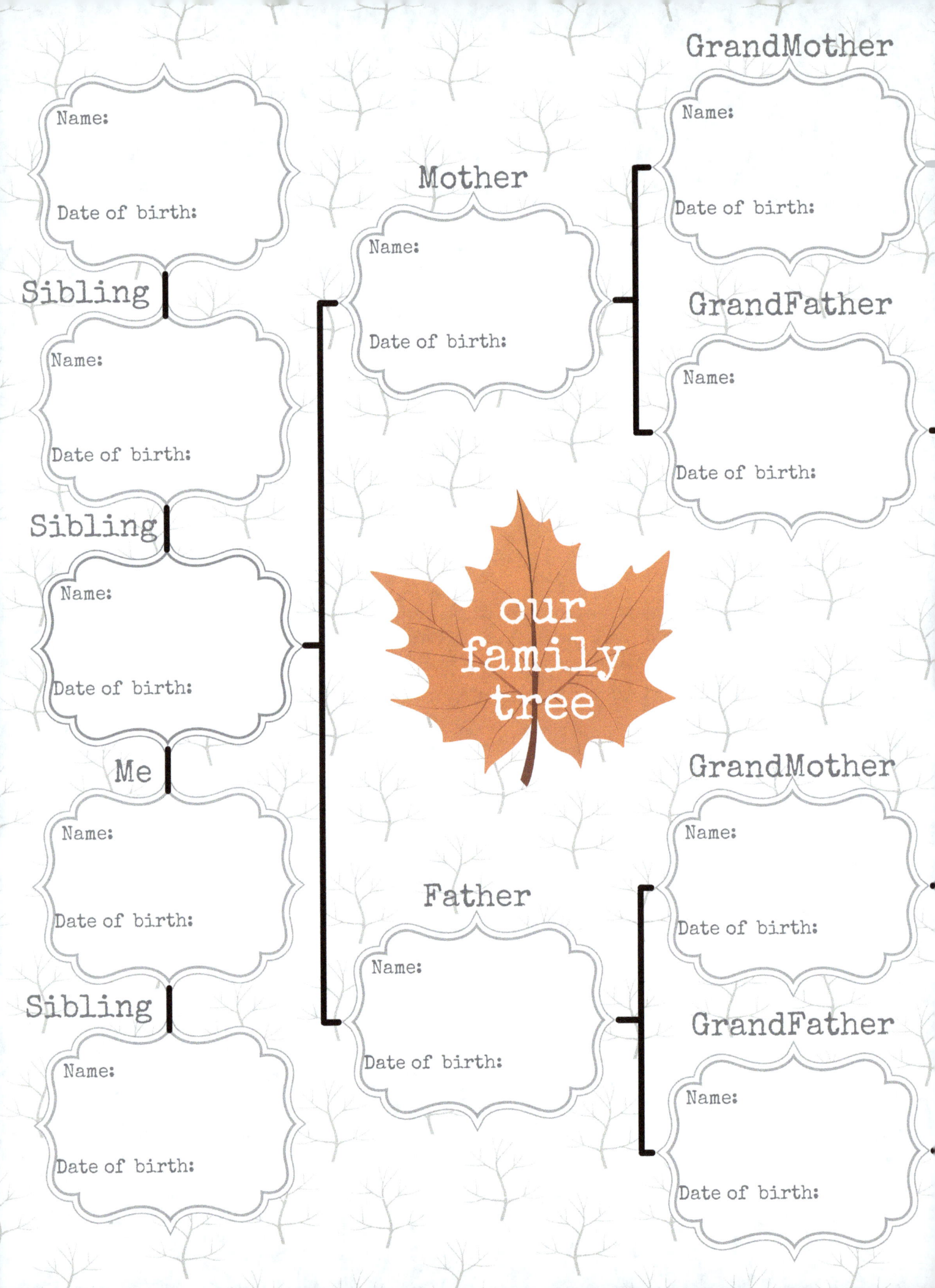

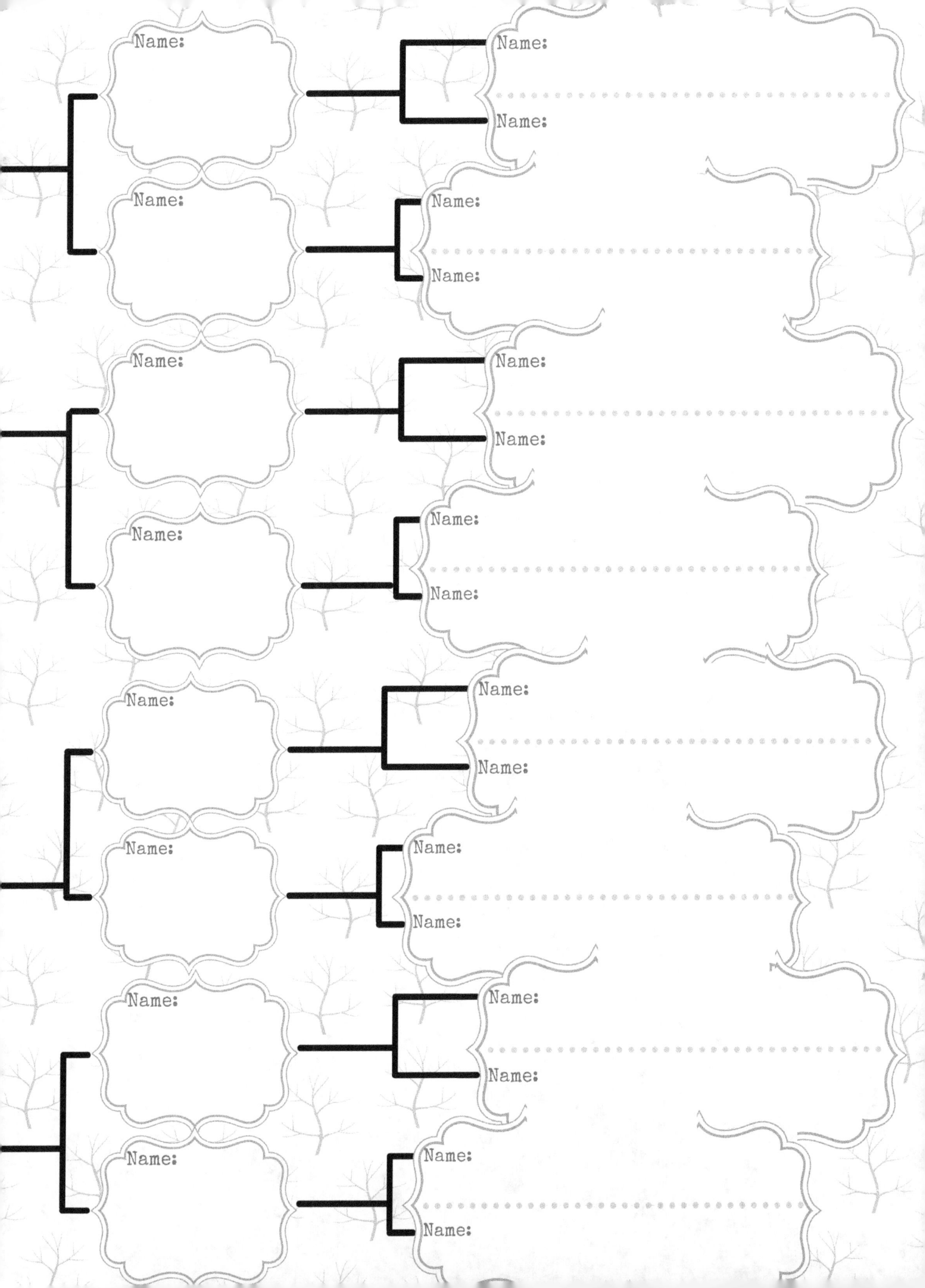

Chapter 1

My Grandmother and Her Family

When were you born?

- When were you born? Were you born in a hospital, at home or elsewhere?

- Full Name

- Date of birth

- Place of birth

- Eye color

- Hair color

- Distinguishing marks

- Where you named after anyone, maybe a family member?

- Does your name have a special meaning?

- Do you like or dislike your name? Why is that?

- What did your mom call you? Did she use different names when she was angry? What about when she was proud or happy?

- Do you have a nickname that your siblings or friends called you?

- How did you get the nickname?

- If you could choose a different name, what would it be? Why?

- How old were your parents when you were born?

- Are there any stories you were told about your birth?

- Where you a healthy baby, or were there health concerns? What were you suffering from?

- What is the earliest memory that you have? Tell me more.

- Did you have siblings? What are their names and how old were they when you were born?

- Did you fight with your siblings? Why? What about?

- What did your family do for fun when you were a kid?

Grandma do you have any photo of you as a baby?

Please glue a photo here, if there is any.

About my grandmother's parents

- What are the names of your parents and where were they born? Do you know where each of them were born?

- How many children were in your family? What are their full names?

- Could you tell me a story or a special memory about your brothers and sisters? What did you like to do with your brothers and sisters?

- What were the occupations of your parents?

- What were your parent's favorite activities after they retired? Why?

- How did your family spend time together when you were young?

- What is the most important lesson that your parents taught you?

- What do you remember most about your mother?

- What is your favorite memory about your mother?

- What do you remember most about your father?

- Tell me about your favorite memory with your father.

Grandma do you have any photo of your parents?

Please glue a photo here, if there is any.

About my grandmother's grandparents (My Great-greats!)

- What were your grandparents like?

- What is your favorite memory of your grandparents?

- How did your grandparents earn their living?

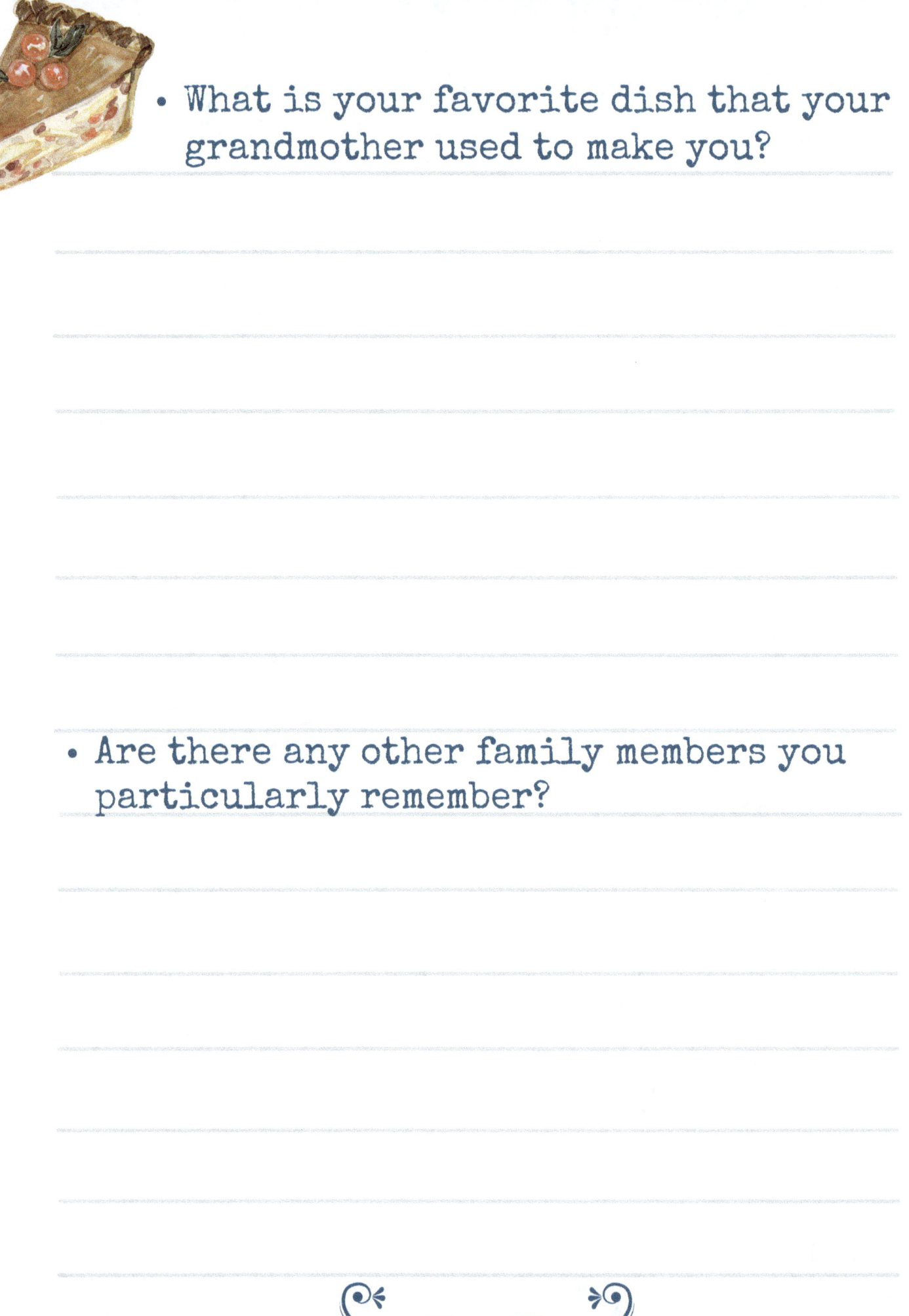

- What is your favorite dish that your grandmother used to make you?

- Are there any other family members you particularly remember?

- What makes them stand out in your mind?

Grandma do you have any photo of your grandparents?

Please glue a photo here, if there is any.

Grandma do you have any photo of your favorite family member?

Please glue a photo here, if there is any.

Chapter 2

My Grandmother Growing Up

About my grandmother's home

- Where did you grow up?

_____

_____

_____

- What was your hometown like?

_____

_____

_____

_____

_____

- What was your neighborhood like?

- What are your earliest memories about your first home?

- What about other homes and places you lived?

Grandma do you have any photo of your house?

Please glue a photo here, if there is any.

Grandmother as a child

- What was your favorite toy or activity as a child?

- What was your favorite pet when you were a child?

- What was one of your favorite shows as a child?

- What do you like to watch now?

- What's one of your favorite memories from childhood?

- What kind of chores did you do as a kid?

- Did you get good grades?

- What was your favorite subject and who was your favorite teacher in school?

- What did you not like to eat as a kid?

- What kind of books did you like to read?

- What did you want to be when you grew up?

- What's one of your favorite activities now?

Grandma do you have any photo of you as a child?

Please glue a photo here, if there is any.

When grandma was a teen

- What was your favorite activity as a teen?

Did you go to school; high school; college or trade/technical school?

- Did you get an allowance? How much was it and what did you spend your money on?

- What was the most rebellious thing you did when you were young?

- Did you ever get into trouble as a child or teenager? Why? Tell me more.

- Did you have a curfew and what time was it? Did you ever miss curfew? What was your parents' reaction? Did you get punished? How?

- What did your friends do for fun when you were young?

- Did you have a best friend? What was his/her name and what do you remember doing most of the time you were together?

- When you were young, did you ever collect anything? What happened to your collection? Do you still have it?

- Can you name one memory with your best friend?

- Do you remember your first kiss?

- Who was your first date? Do you remember their name? Where did you meet? Tell me more about your first date.

Grandma do you have any photo of you as a teen?

Please glue a photo here, if there is any.

Chapter 3

Grandma Becoming An Adult

Grandma on her own

- What's the best place you've traveled to?

- What is your favorite city to visit?

- Do you have a favorite family vacation memory? Why is this your favorite?

- Do you practice a religion? What impact has religion had on your life?

- What is your favorite color?

- What is your favorite dish?

- What are your favorite book, movie, and song?

- What's the best advice someone's ever given you?

Grandma do you have any photo of you as a young adult?

Please glue a photo here, if there is any.

Grandma's early career

- Have you had a summer job?

- What was your first job?

- How did you decide on a career? What/who had a great role in choosing your career?

- Did you have a car? What was your first car?

- What age were you at that time and who bought the car for you?

Grandma do you have any photo of you working?

Please glue a photo here, if there is any.

Grandma's love and marriage

- How did you meet grandpa? Tell me about that.

- What is your favorite thing about grandpa?

- What was your marriage proposal like? Was he a romantic boyfriend?

- Where was your wedding? Who was your maid of honor/ matron of honor/best man?

- What is the best memory that you remember regarding your wedding day?

- Have you been married more than once? Can you tell me more about your other marriages?

- If you could turn back time, would you still marry grandpa?

- What do you think is the most important thing in being married?

- If I was getting married tomorrow, what is your advice/ words of wisdom for me?

Grandma do you have any photo from your wedding that you want to show me?

Please glue a photo here, if there is any.

Where grandma lived

- Where did you lived as newlyweds?

- Tell me more about the places you lived together before buying your first house.

- Tell me about your first house (did you have kids, how did you find the house, how did you pay for it, what did you like about that house?)

- If you could have lived in a different place, where would it be?

- If you could have lived in a different era, when would it be?

- If you could travel into space, would you?

- What's your favorite technological invention that occurred in your lifetime?

- Do you have any regrets?

- If you were to start your life over, what would you do differently?

Grandma do you have any photo of you and grandpa before having kids?

Please glue a photo here, if there is any.

Grandma do you have any photo with your house?

Please glue a photo here, if there is any.

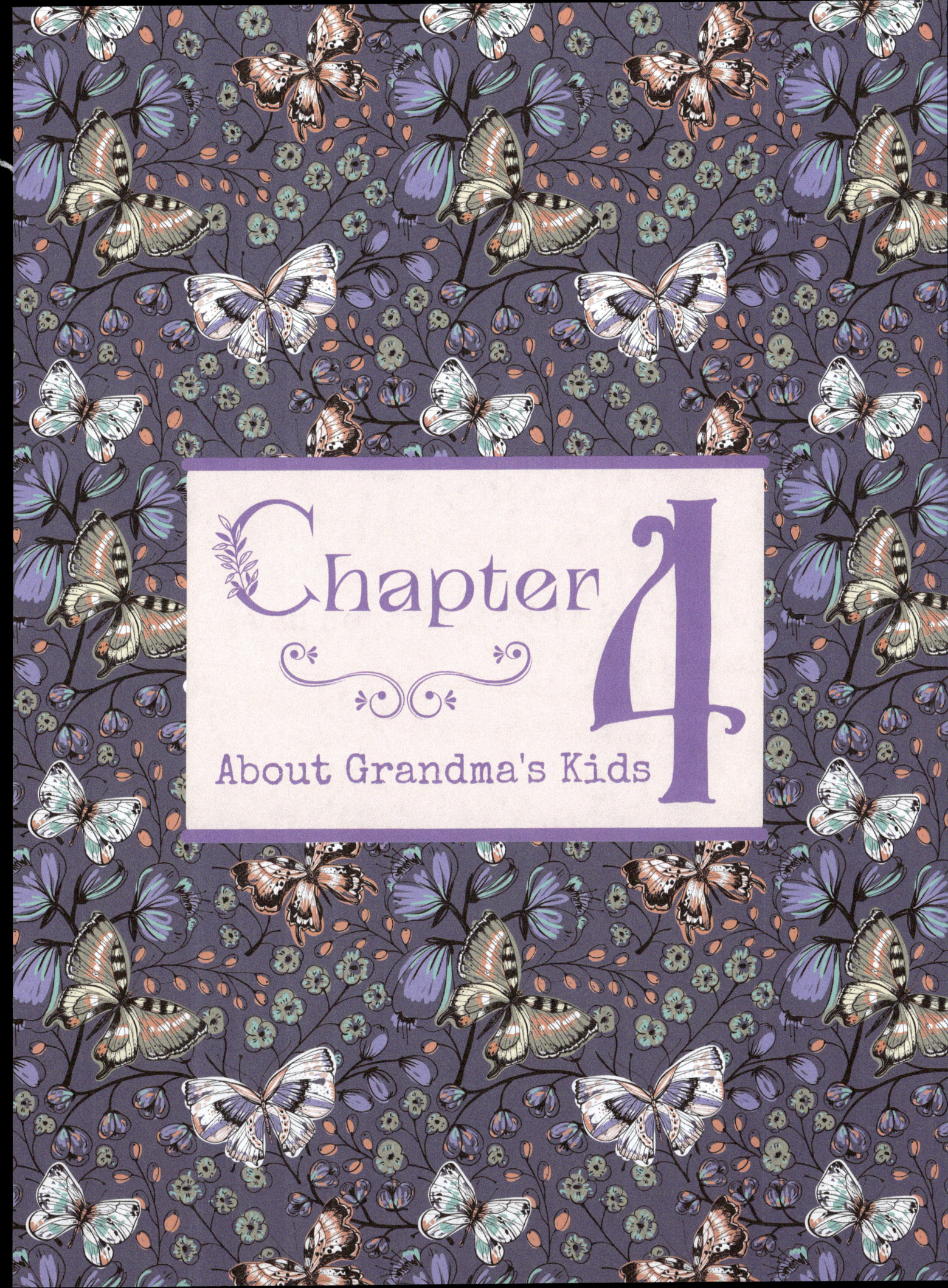

Grandma's kids: my parent, my aunts, and uncles

- How many children did you have alltogether?

_____
_____
_____
_____
_____
_____

- What are their names, birth dates and birthplaces?

- Why did you give my parent this name?

Grandma do you have any photo with all your kids altogether?

Please glue a photo here, if there is any.

Grandma do you have any photo of you and all your kids altogether?

Please glue a photo here, if there is any.

When my parent was born

- Grandma, tell me about the day when my parent was born?

- What's one of your favorite memories of being a mom?

- What was most rewarding about being a parent?

- What is your favorite memory with my parent?

Grandma do you have any photo from the day my parent was born?

Please glue a photo here, if there is any.

When my parent was a child

- Tell me a naughty story about my parent?

- Are there any funny things about your children that stands out?

- Did my parent have a favorite toy?

- What was one thing that my parent did that made you feel proud?

- What was one thing that my parent did that made you the maddest, and why?

- What did you do for fun when my parent was a kid?

Grandma do you have any photo of my parent as a child?

Please glue a photo here, if there is any.

About my parent's education

- What did my parent wanted to be when he/she grew up?

- Where you strict or lenient as a parent?

- What were the rules you had in your household?

- What were the chores my parent was responsible for?

- Was my parent good at doing chores? Was my parent a responsible kid?

Grandma do you have any photo from my parent graduation day?

Please glue a photo here, if there is any.

About my parent's family life

- What is the funniest family story you remember?

- How did my parents meet?

- What was your first impression when you meet my other parent?

- Has my parent owned any pets? What was their first pet?

- If animals could talk, what would the pet say about my parent?

- What was the hardest choice my parent had to made?

Grandma do you have any photo with my parents before I was born?

Please glue a photo here, if there is any.

Chapter 5

Family Traditions

Our family gatherings

- What type of events do our family gather for?

_____

_____

_____

_____

_____

_____

_____

- Do you have a preferred holiday? Which one and why?

- What is your favorite thing about this holiday?

- Who is always arriving late to family gatherings?

- Is there any special tradition that our family keeps when gathering?

Grandma do you have any photo with our family gathering?

Please glue a photo here, if there is any.

- What is your favorite family recipe?

- From whom did you get it?

- What are the best traditional dishes you cook for different events like Christmas, Easter, New Year, etc.?

- What is my parent's favorite recipe?

Recipe for _____

NAME OF DISH

FROM THE KITCHEN OF

_____

 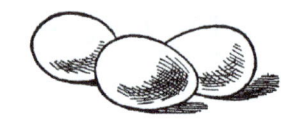

INGREDIENTS

SERVES

PREP TIME

TOTAL TIME

OVEN TEMP

DIRECTIONS

Recipe for

NAME OF DISH

DIRECTIONS

NOTES / POSSIBLE IMPROVEMENTS:

Recipe for _____

FROM THE KITCHEN OF
_____

NAME OF DISH

INGREDIENTS

SERVES _____

PREP TIME _____

TOTAL TIME _____

OVEN TEMP _____

DIRECTIONS

Recipe for

NAME OF DISH

DIRECTIONS

NOTES / POSSIBLE IMPROVEMENTS:

Recipe for _____
NAME OF DISH

FROM THE KITCHEN OF

_____

SERVES _____

PREP TIME _____

TOTAL TIME _____

OVEN TEMP _____

INGREDIENTS

DIRECTIONS

Recipe for

NAME OF DISH

DIRECTIONS

NOTES / POSSIBLE IMPROVEMENTS:

Recipe for _____

NAME OF DISH

FROM THE KITCHEN OF

_____

SERVES _____

PREP TIME _____

TOTAL TIME _____

OVEN TEMP _____

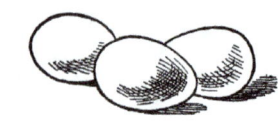

INGREDIENTS

DIRECTIONS

Recipe for

NAME OF DISH

DIRECTIONS

NOTES / POSSIBLE IMPROVEMENTS:

Recipe for

NAME OF DISH

FROM THE KITCHEN OF

INGREDIENTS

SERVES

PREP TIME

TOTAL TIME

OVEN TEMP

 DIRECTIONS

Recipe for _____

NAME OF DISH

DIRECTIONS

NOTES / POSSIBLE IMPROVEMENTS:

Chapter 6

About Life and Living

Historic events in grandma's lifetime

- What were the most memorable historic events that happened during your life?

Grandma's wisdom

- What are you thankful for?

- What makes you happy?

- How do you handle stress? Are you easily annoyed?

- Is there anything left on your bucket list?

- Do you have a favorite age/stage in your life?

- Are there any secrets to living a long, fulfilling life?

- What could you tell me that I would be surprised to learn about you?

Grandma can you show me a recent photo of you ?

Please glue a photo here, if there is any.

- If you could be a superhero, what's a magic ability you'd like to have for the rest of your life?

- What's a rule that you'd make everyone follow?

- What scares you the most?

- What is your dream for your children and grandchildren?

- What is the biggest difference about growing up today than when you were a child?

- What is your favorite thing about being a grandparent?

- What's one of your favorite memories of being a grandma?

Grandma do you have any photo with your grandkids?

Please glue a photo here, if there is any.

Family traits grandma sees in me

- What family traits do you see in me?

Grandma's wishes for me